ROBOTS from Then to Now

BY RACHEL GRACK

SEQUENCE

AMICUS | AMICUS INK

Sequence is published by Amicus and Amicus Ink
P.O. Box 1329, Mankato, MN 56002
www.amicuspublishing.us

Library of Congress Cataloging-in-Publication Data
Names: Koestler-Grack, Rachel A., 1973- author.
Title: Robots from then to now / by Rachel Grack.
Description: Mankato, Minnesota : Amicus/Amicus Ink, [2020] |
Series: Sequence developments in technology | Includes bibliographical references and index. | Audience: Grade 4 to 6.
Identifiers: LCCN 2018048685 (print) | LCCN 2018050829 (ebook) | ISBN 9781681517674 (pdf) | ISBN 9781681516851 (library binding) | ISBN 9781681524719 (paperback)
Subjects: LCSH: Robots--History--Juvenile literature.
Classification: LCC TJ211.2 (ebook) | LCC TJ211.2 .K64 2020 (print) | DDC 629.8/9209--dc23
LC record available at https://lccn.loc.gov/2018048685

Editor: Wendy Dieker
Designer: Aubrey Harper
Photo Researcher: Holly Young

Photo Credits: Taavi Burns/Flickr cover; KOHb/iStock cover; Mary Evans Picture Library Ltd/Age Fotostock 4; trade card by unnamed artist/Mary Evans 7; Hulton Archive/Getty 8; SSPL/Getty Images/Getty 11; National Institute of Standards and Technology Digital Collections, Gaithersburg, MD 20899/WikiCommons 12–13; Eye Ubiquitous/Alamy 15; AlesiaKan/Shutterstock 16; Craig Durling/ZUMA Wire/Alamy 18–19; Yoshikazu Tsuno/AFP/Getty 20; Handout/KRT/Newscom 22–23; Softbank Robotics Europe/WikiCommons 24; Yonhap News/YNA/Newscom 27; Nuro/Kroger/Cover Images/Newscom 28–29

Printed in the United States of America

HC 10 9 8 7 6 5 4 3 2 1
PB 10 9 8 7 6 5 4 3 2 1

TABLE OF CONTENTS

LOADING...LOADING...LOADING...

Incredible Robots

People have always been interested in robots. From ancient times, people told stories of machines that could move on their own. Inventors tried new things. And finally, machines could really move all by themselves! Robots have changed from then to now. They do more and more things on their own.

A science fiction magazine from 1934 features a robot on the cover.

LOADING . . . LOADING . . . LOADING . . .

Some of the very first moving machines were **automatons**. These machines did a series of set movements. Inside were gears and springs like a clock. In 1739, inventor Jacques de Vaucanson built many of these fun machines. His most famous was a duck. It could eat, quack, and flap its wings. But people really enjoyed watching it poop!

Vaucanson built all kinds of useful machines. His duck was just for fun.

Jacques de Vaucanson builds the duck automaton.

1739

. . LOADING . . . LOADING .

ADING . . . LOADING . . . LOADING . . .

A cellist plays music while ELEKTRO moves his arms like he's conducting.

Jacques de Vaucanson builds the duck automaton.

1739

1939

ELEKTRO wows crowds at the World's Fair.

LOADING . . . LOADING

For 200 years, people tried to make machines that could really move and think on their own. In 1939, ELEKTRO was unveiled at the **World's Fair** in New York. It was 7 feet (2.1 m) tall. It could answer questions and tell jokes. It could even follow simple voice commands. People wondered what else robots could do.

LOADING . . . LOADING . . . LOADING . . .

Robots at Work

In 1948, Dr. W. Grey Walter was studying the human brain. Dr. Walter built a robot turtle. It could move by itself. If it ran into something, it would go a different direction. The robot's **sensors** sent messages to the motors. Dr. Walter could see how our brains get messages from our senses, just like the robot's motor.

1739 — Jacques de Vaucanson builds the duck automaton.

1939 — ELEKTRO wows crowds at the World's Fair.

1948 — Dr. W. Grey Walter studies the brain using robot turtles.

G . . . LOADING

Dr. Walter built a robot to study how electronic messages go from sensors to the motors.

LOADING...LOADING...LOADING...

Jacques de Vaucanson builds the duck automaton.

Dr. W. Grey Walter studies the brain using robot turtles.

1739 1939 1948 1954 LOADING

ELEKTRO wows crowds at the World's Fair.

George Devol builds the first factory robot.

In the meantime, workers wanted to use robots to make jobs easier. Maybe robots could help build things. In 1954, George Devol built a robot arm. It could move parts around at a factory. He called it Unimate. It did boring factory jobs, over and over. Work got done faster.

Researchers use a Unimate arm to study how robots can do factory work.

Robots proved to be useful in science and in factories. But could robot workers look like people? In 1973 in Japan, Ichiro Kato built the first robot that moved like a person. WABOT's computer mind could think! It could see and hear. It could even speak. But WABOT actually looked more like a machine than a person.

WABOT 2 was built seven years after the first one. With better fingers, it could play a keyboard.

1739 — Jacques de Vaucanson builds the duck automaton.

1939 — ELEKTRO wows crowds at the World's Fair.

1948 — Dr. W. Grey Walter studies the brain using robot turtles.

1954 — George Devol builds the first factory robot.

1973 — Ichiro Kato creates the world's first human-like robot.

OADING . . . LOADING . . . LOADING . . .

1739	1939	1948	1954	1973	1998
Jacques de Vaucanson builds the duck automaton.	ELEKTRO wows crowds at the World's Fair.	Dr. W. Grey Walter studies the brain using robot turtles.	George Devol builds the first factory robot.	Ichiro Kato creates the world's first human-like robot.	Lego creates its MindStorms line of robot toys.

Robots at Home

Robots can be complicated. Not just anybody can make one. Or could they? In 1998, Lego starting selling a robot kit. The MindStorms kit came with a small computer and little motors. Kids used sensors and Lego bricks to build a creature or vehicle. They **programmed** the computer with instructions for the robot. These simple robots would do tasks on their own.

The Lego EV3 kit lets even kids build and program a robot.

OADING . . . LOADING . . . LOADING . . .

Sony also wanted to make robot toys. In 1999, they released robot puppies to play with. Named Aibo, these little dogs could bark and wag their tails. They could chase a ball. In 2018, an updated pooch was released. Today, Aibo knows some new tricks. It reacts to smiles, recognizes its family, and learns where rooms are in the house.

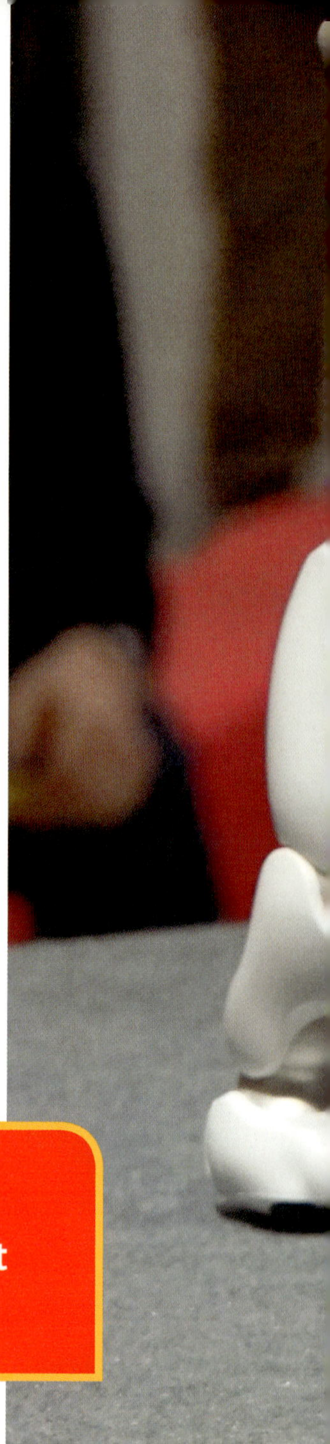

Cameras in Aibo's face send messages to its computer. The robot reacts almost like a real dog.

1739	Jacques de Vaucanson builds the duck automaton.
1939	ELEKTRO wows crowds at the World's Fair.
1948	Dr. W. Grey Walter studies the brain using robot turtles.
1954	George Devol builds the first factory robot.
1973	Ichiro Kato creates the world's first human-like robot.
1998	Lego creates its MindStorms line of robot toys.

1999

LOADING . . . LOADING . . .

Sony creates a robot dog named Aibo.

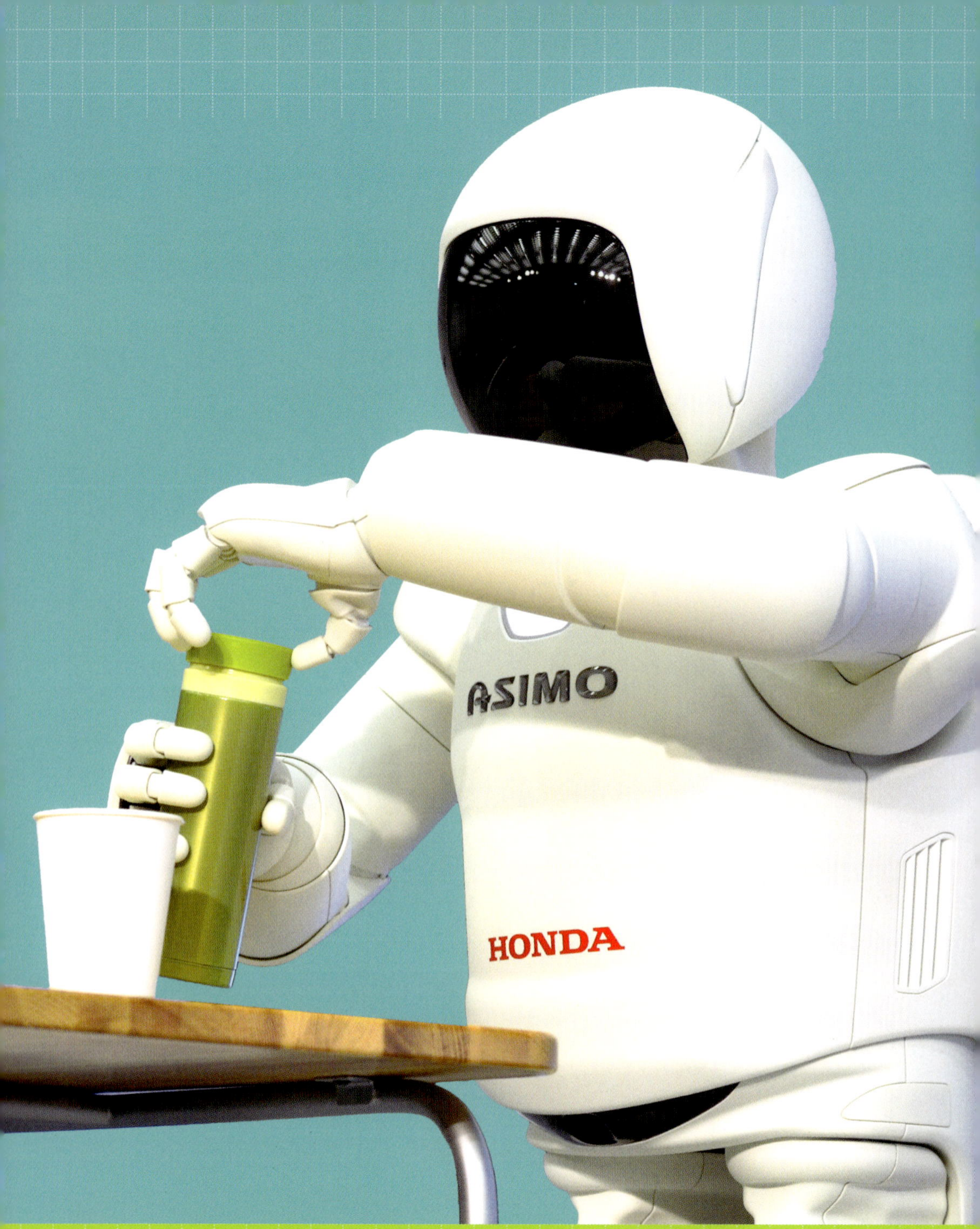

1739	1939	1948	1954	1973	1998
Jacques de Vaucanson builds the duck automaton.	ELEKTRO wows crowds at the World's Fair.	Dr. W. Grey Walter studies the brain using robot turtles.	George Devol builds the first factory robot.	Ichiro Kato creates the world's first human-like robot.	Lego creates its MindStorms line of robot toys.

Robot Helpers

Inventors keep working to find ways for robots to help people. The Honda Motor Company built ASIMO in 2000. They want ASIMO to help people in the home. Today this robot can run and climb stairs. Its fingers can turn on light switches. It can even do **sign language**. It learns voices and faces.

ASIMO's fingers can twist a cap off of a bottle.

ASIMO is introduced.

1999 | 2000 | ING . . . LOADING . . .

Sony creates a robot dog named Aibo.

The iRobot robotics company decided it was time to get some housework done! In 2002, they built a helpful home robot called Roomba. Roomba is a robot vacuum cleaner. It rolls from room to room, under and around furniture. Time for a break? Roombas return to their **docking stations** and recharge.

Roombas can be programmed to clean floors when no one is home.

- 1739 — Jacques de Vaucanson builds the duck automaton.
- 1939 — ELEKTRO wows crowds at the World's Fair.
- 1948 — Dr. W. Grey Walter studies the brain using robot turtles.
- 1954 — George Devol builds the first factory robot.
- 1973 — Ichiro Kato creates the world's first human-like robot.
- 1998 — Lego creates its MindStorms line of robot toys.

ASIMO is introduced.

1999 — Sony creates a robot dog named Aibo.

2000 — ASIMO is introduced.

2002 — iRobot Roomba starts vacuuming floors by itself.

. . . LOADING . . .

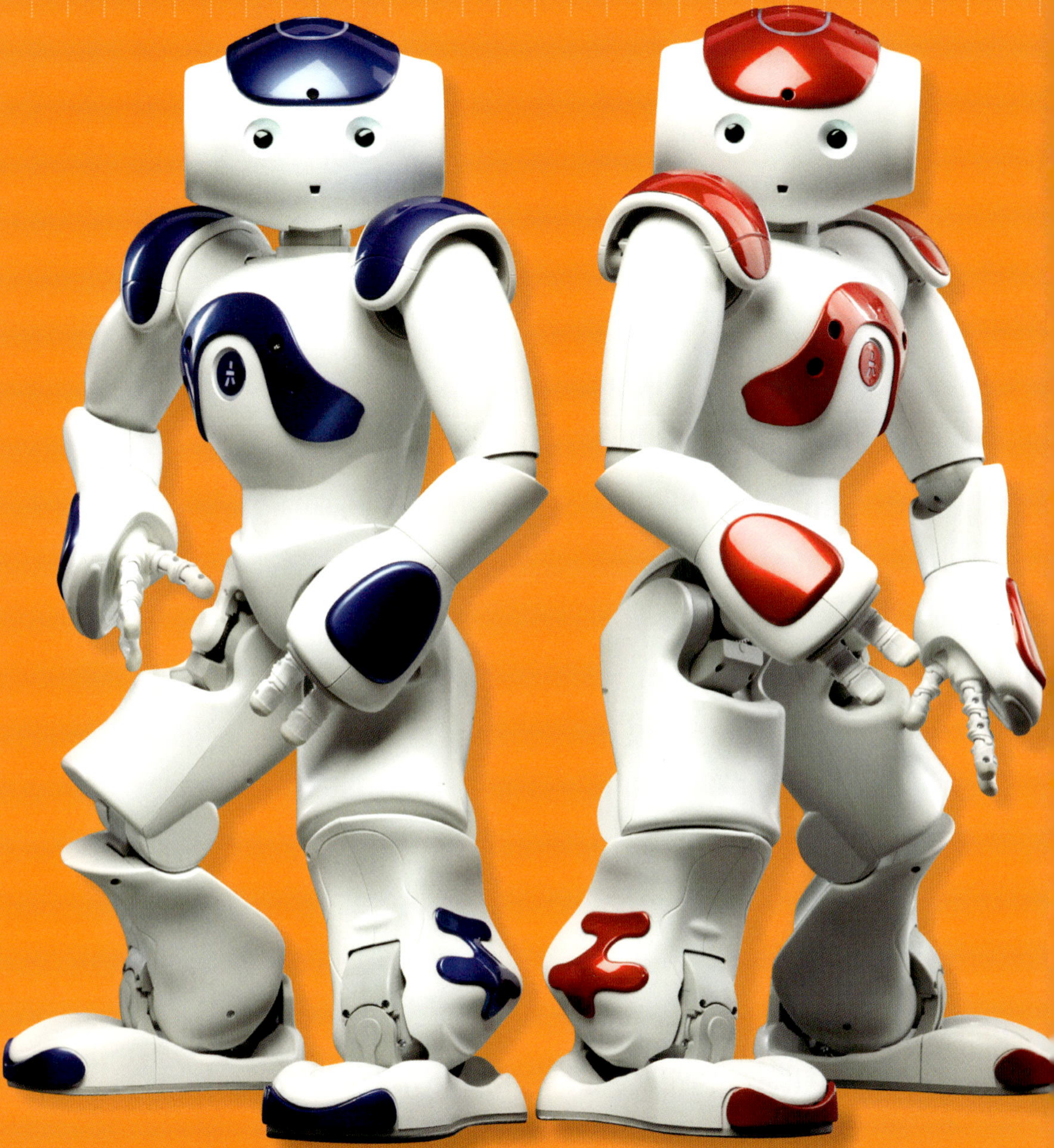

1739 — Jacques de Vaucanson builds the duck automaton.

1939 — ELEKTRO wows crowds at the World's Fair.

1948 — Dr. W. Grey Walter studies the brain using robot turtles.

1954 — George Devol builds the first factory robot.

1973 — Ichiro Kato creates the world's first human-like robot.

1998 — Lego creates its MindStorms line of robot toys.

Can a robot help in school? Yes, it can! In 2004, robot builders invented the NAO robot. In 2008, schools brought in this little **humanoid** to help in the classroom. Some students learned programming and robotics. But some children with special needs found a friend in NAO. NAO can talk with kids. They can have fun learning from a cute robot.

NAO robots are only about 2 feet (58 cm) tall. They look friendly and helpful.

- 1999 — Sony creates a robot dog named Aibo.
- 2000 — ASIMO is introduced.
- 2002 — iRobot Roomba starts vacuuming floors by itself.
- 2008 — NAO robots start helping in classrooms.

ADING . . .

South Korea has plenty of robot workers. They were on display in the 2018 Winter Olympics there. One lucky robot named HUBO even got to pass the torch! HUBO is a **rescue** robot. He was one of 85 robots at the 2018 Winter Olympics. The robots were there to work. They served as police officers and cleaners.

HUBO receives the Olympic torch for the 2018 Winter Olympics in South Korea.

- **1739** Jacques de Vaucanson builds the duck automaton.
- **1939** ELEKTRO wows crowds at the World's Fair.
- **1948** Dr. W. Grey Walter studies the brain using robot turtles.
- **1954** George Devol builds the first factory robot.
- **1973** Ichiro Kato creates the world's first human-like robot.
- **1998** Lego creates its MindStorms line of robot toys.

1999 — Sony creates a robot dog named Aibo.

2000 — ASIMO is introduced.

2002 — iRobot Roomba starts vacuuming floors by itself.

2008 — NAO robots start helping in classrooms.

2018 — Robots work at the Winter Olympics in South Korea.

1739	Jacques de Vaucanson builds the duck automaton.
1939	ELEKTRO wows crowds at the World's Fair.
1948	Dr. W. Grey Walter studies the brain using robot turtles.
1954	George Devol builds the first factory robot.
1973	Ichiro Kato creates the world's first human-like robot.
1998	Lego creates its MindStorms line of robot toys.

Into the Future!

What will people see robots doing next? How about delivering groceries? One grocery store uses Nuro **self-driving cars**. People order groceries. A worker puts them in the robot car. Then the car finds its own way to the buyer's door. Robots today prove to be much more useful than a pooping duck!

A Nuro robot car drives through a city to make a delivery.

1999 — Sony creates a robot dog named Aibo.

2000 — ASIMO is introduced.

2002 — iRobot Roomba starts vacuuming floors by itself.

2008 — NAO robots start helping in classrooms.

2018 — Robots work at the Winter Olympics in South Korea.

2019 — Self-driving cars deliver groceries to homes.

Glossary

automaton A machine that looks like a person or animal and moves by itself; automatons led to today's robots.

docking station A place to plug in an electronic device so its battery can recharge.

humanoid A robot that is designed to look like a human.

program To enter instructions into a computer to tell a robot what to do

rescue To save something from danger.

self-driving car A vehicle that has no driver; a person programs a destination, and the car finds its own way with GPS, LIDAR, sensors, and cameras.

sensor An instrument that can sense objects, heat, sound, light, and so on.

sign language A language of hand signals and gestures that lets people who can't use vocal language to communicate.

World's Fair A show of each country's new technology and achievements; people come to see demonstrations of new products and ideas over a few days.

Read More

Crane, Cody. *Robots.* New York: Children's Press, 2018.

Higgins, Nadia. *Robots at Home.* Mankato, Minn.: Amicus, 2018.

Swanson, Jennifer. *Everything Robotics.* Washington, D.C.: National Geographic Kids, 2016.

Websites

Easy Science for Kids: All about Robotics

http://easyscienceforkids.com/all-about-robotics

Kiddle: Robot Facts for Kids

https://kids.kiddle.co/Robot

Science Kids: History of Robotics

www.sciencekids.co.nz/sciencefacts/technology/historyofrobotics.html

Every effort has been made to ensure that these websites are appropriate for children. However, because of the nature of the Internet, it is impossible to guarantee that these sites will remain active indefinitely or that their contents will not be altered.

Index

About the Author

Rachel Grack has worked in children's nonfiction publishing since 1999. Rachel lives on a small desert ranch in Arizona. She enjoys spending time with her family and barnyard of animals. Thanks to our wireless world, her ranch stays tapped into developing technology.